Wallis C. Metts, PhD, who teaches journalism at Spring Arbor University, has won awards from the Educational Press Association for writing and editing for children. His book credits include *Inspirations for Daily Living, Promises of the Bible, Daily Prayer Book: Prayers for Our Country,* and *Children's Book of the Bible.* He and his wife raise Christmas trees and barn cats on a small farm in southern Michigan. His seven grandchildren call him Santa.

Front Cover Images: Thinkstock

Back Cover Images: Thinkstock

Interior Illustrations: Thomas Gianni, Randall Hamblin, Michael Jaroszko, Victoria and Julius Lisi, Lyn Martin, Karen Pritchett, Sally Schaedler, James E. Seward, Gary Torrisi

Interior Photos: iStockphoto, Zev Radovan, Shutterstock.com, Thinkstock

ISBN-13: 978-1-4508-5459-7
ISBN-10: 1-4508-5459-1

Manufactured in China.

8 7 6 5 4 3 2 1

KIDS—WELCOME TO YOUR FIRST BIBLE DICTIONARY.

Have you ever wondered what it was like to live in Bible times? Do you know what people ate or wore? Do you know who wrote the Bible, when those people lived, and what they did? This book helps you understand the people of the Bible and how they lived. You will find out what many of the words in the Bible mean. And you will find lots of pictures that help you understand.

If you know your ABC's, you can find words because a dictionary puts words in order of their first letter. What this means is that just like the alphabet, all of the words that begin with the letter *A* come first, and then those that start with the letter *B* are next. The words that begin with *Z* come at the very end of the dictionary. Just look for the large letters or the two *guide words* at the top of the page.

Guide words show the first and last words on that page, and they also show where the words are in the alphabet. You may also notice that all of the letters of the alphabet are in order on the side of each page. This is to help you if you need to know which letters come before or after each other in alphabetical order when you are looking up words in the dictionary. There will be a big arrow next to the starting letter of words featured on a given page. Of course, you can also read any page just for fun. There are no stories here, but this dictionary can help you better understand the stories in the Bible.

As you explore your new dictionary, try to connect these words and pictures to what you already know about the Bible from church or Sunday school. Ask your parents, grandparents, and teachers to tell you what they know, too.

The Bible is one of the most important books in the whole world. And this dictionary can help you understand and enjoy it.

A B C D E F G H I J K L M N O P Q R S T U V W X Y Z

Parents, grandparents, and teachers—

Noah Webster, who put together the first American dictionary, learned 26 languages in order to make sure he understood the history of the 70,000 words he included. It was a monumental work of scholarship—but Webster believed a dictionary was not merely the work of scholars. He said it was "something arising out of the work, needs, ties, joys, affections and tastes of long generations of humanity." From that day to this, hardly any home would be caught without a reliable dictionary—a key tool for understanding language and culture. *My First Bible Dictionary* is much smaller and much simpler than Webster's work, but this dictionary also arises from the

ties and joys of our long affection for and deep faith in the Bible—a book that has maintained its place of honor in many homes for hundreds of years.

Designed to be used by young readers, *My First Bible Dictionary* introduces them to the richness of this remarkable book. Here children will find information about people and daily life in Bible times. They'll learn about foods, tools, clothes, and many details about Jesus' miracles and parables. This information can provide insight into the stories of the Bible and help unlock our understanding today.

As much as possible, this dictionary helps young readers understand words in simple terms. Chronology and context are difficult concepts for young children, but as much as possible these are explained or illustrated. Sentences that use the terms are often included immediately after the definitions, helping to make their meaning more clear.

The Bible itself covers several thousand years of human history. It is a compilation of countless stories from many generations, rich in history, drama, and inspiration. Over this long period of time, some of the items used by people of the Bible—such as clothing or weapons, for example— have changed. In other topics, such as animals, many simply went by much different names than we are used to. In addition, the daily lives of the people described in Genesis were considerably different than that experienced by those in the Gospels. Therefore, distinctions between Old and New Testament terms are frequent and useful. *Earlier* and *later* are terms that do not do justice to the breadth of biblical history, but they are sufficient for young minds.

Several principles governed the selection of words for this volume. No effort was made to explain theology, of course, but simple definitions of key terms such as "grace" and "salvation" are provided. Many words were chosen because they could be illustrated easily and provide knowledge about subjects that children generally find interesting—foods, clothing, tools, weapons, animals, and other objects used in Bible times.

Because the King James Version is still highly regarded and commonly available, a number of words from that translation are included as well. This includes many words that are no longer used or meanings that have changed.

The King James Version is often quoted, and young readers may also find its language in books and stories they read throughout their lives.

My First Bible Dictionary is an exciting tool to help children find out more about the Bible. Remember that children learn best with the help of adults such as parents and teachers, so be ready to step in to assist if children ask for or need help.

This handy Bible reference also opens the door to many useful ideas—ideas that have been foundational to United States history and law. Shortly after he finished his dictionary in 1828, Webster went on to write *The History of the United States*, one of our earliest textbooks. In this early and influential textbook he wrote that our civic virtues are rooted in the Christian faith. "The Bible was America's textbook in all fields," he observed.

And it is still essential to a complete education.

A B C D E F G H I J K L M N O P Q R S T U V W X Y Z

Aaron

The first high priest in Israel. **Aaron** was the brother of Moses.

abase

To **abase** is to lower. Usually it means to be shamed or to think less of ourselves.

abate

To recede or reduce. The floodwaters **abated.**

abba

An affectionate word for father, like daddy or papa.

Abel

A son of Adam and Eve, the first parents. He was killed by his brother Cain.

abhor

If you hate something because it is so horrible, you **abhor** it.

abide

Your home is the place you **abide.** You **abide** where you feel comfortable and safe.

Abigail

One of King David's wives. She was beautiful and wise.

abomination

An **abomination** is something so sinful we don't like to even think about it.

Abraham

Abraham was the father of the Hebrews. He believed and followed God, who told him to move to a new country. God also promised him that he would have many children.

abstain

To **abstain** is to choose not to do something, usually something bad.

abyss

Something so deep no one knows where the bottom is. A pit or ocean can be an **abyss.**

accord

When everyone agrees, they are in **accord.**

account

To give reasons for or to explain your actions. A record of the money one owes is also an **account.**

accuse

When you blame someone for something that goes wrong, you **accuse** him or her.

acknowledge

Recognize or agree with. You can **acknowledge** a person or an idea.

acre

An **acre** is the amount of land an ox can plow in a single day. It is a way to describe how much land one owns or plows.

Acts

A book in the Bible that tells the story of the apostles and the first Christian churches.

Adam

The first man. God made **Adam** out of dust and breathed life into him.

adder

A kind of poisonous snake.

admonish

To recommend or suggest. Usually we **admonish** someone to do the right thing.

adopt

To choose someone or something as your own. Parents may **adopt** a child who has no parents.

adultery

Adultery is when a married man sleeps with a woman who is not his wife or a married woman sleeps with a man who is not her husband.

adversary

An enemy. God protects his people from their **adversaries.**

A B C D E F G H I J K L M N O P Q R S T U V W X Y Z

advocate

A person who helps or comforts you by taking your side is an **advocate.**

afflict

To cause pain, distress, or grief. That pain is an **affliction.**

age

Usually a long period of time. God is the king of all **ages,** all periods of time.

alabaster

A light-colored stone used to make boxes or vases for perfume, oils, or cream. Her box was made of **alabaster.**

alas

Alas is a word to use when you are sad, afraid, or concerned. It means "Oh, no!" or "Pay attention!"

alien

Someone or something strange. **Alien** is often used to describe someone from another country.

alm

An **alm** is money you give to a poor person. God expects his people to help others who are poor or weak.

almighty

Almighty means God is powerful and in control.

almond

A kind of tree. The nut that grows on the tree is also called an **almond.**

altar

An **altar** was a stack of large stones where people gave things they valued to God. Sometimes they would kill an animal or pour oil on the altar.

ambassador

An **ambassador** represents someone, usually a ruler or king.

amen

If you agree with a prayer or sermon, you say **amen.** It means "yes, that's true."

Amos

A famous shepherd who warned people to worship God and to help take care of poor people. You can read about him in the book of **Amos.**

UNUSUAL ANIMALS IN THE BIBLE

Because the Bible was written long ago, sometimes we don't know what **animal** was being named. Here are some of the most unusual ones—and our best guesses about what they were.

basilisk

A yellow snake, about ten feet long, with a spot on its head that looked like a crown. The name means "king serpent." Also called a cockatrice.

behemoth

A large creature that lives in or near a swamp. This may have been a hippopotamus.

dragon

A large lizard that lives in the desert.

leviathan

A large sea monster with sharp teeth. It was much larger than a crocodile and had webbed feet.

ossifrage

A large bird that eats small animals. The name means "bone-breaker," because the bird drops its food on rocks to break the bones so the bird can eat the food more easily.

pygarg

A white, deerlike creature with twisted horns. It was hunted as food.

satyr

A creature that was part man and part goat. The Hebrews may have used the word to refer to an idol that looked like a goat.

unicorn

A large, fierce animal. It had two horns and could not be tamed. It may have been the oryx.

A B C D E F G H I J K L M N O P Q R S T U V W X Y Z

angel

An **angel** is a messenger from God. These spirit beings are beautiful, wise, and powerful.

anger

Anger is the feeling of being very upset. God is sometimes **angry,** but only at sin.

annunciation

An announcement. An angel told Mary she would be the mother of Jesus. This is called the **Annunciation.**

anoint

When someone was asked to do a special task, like become a priest or king, they were **anointed.** Someone, usually a high priest, would pour oil on their head to show they had been chosen.

anvil

A metal block with a hard, flat top. A hammer is used to pound other metals into tools or weapons on the **anvil.**

anxiety

If you are afraid or worried, you have **anxiety.**

apostle

Someone sent to do special work or give a message. Jesus had special followers who were **apostles.**

archangel

A chief angel, or messenger. Michael is an **archangel.**

ark

A large boat. When God sent a great flood, he told Noah to build an **ark** to save his family and all the animals. It is also the name for a box for holy things.

Ark of the Covenant

A beautiful, gold-covered box used to hold the Ten Commandments and other holy objects. It reminded the Hebrews that God protected them and led them.

armor

The heavy leather or metal clothing soldiers wore in battle is called **armor.** Weapons can also be called armor.

ascension

To *ascend* is to go up. The **Ascension** was when Jesus went back up to heaven.

asleep

When someone died, early Christians would say they were **asleep.**

asp

An **asp** is a poisonous snake, probably a cobra.

assembly

When people gather together for one purpose, they *assemble.* The early church was called an **assembly.**

Assyria

A powerful kingdom that once conquered the Northern Kingdom of Israel.

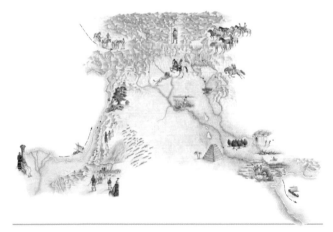

astray

If you get off the path you planned, or God planned, you go **astray.**

atonement

To cover up or cancel is to *atone.* The **atonement** refers to how God cancels the punishment for his people's sins.

Augustus

A title of honor for the first Roman Emperor, Octavian. He was the emperor when Jesus was born.

avenge

To get even with someone for doing something wrong to you or someone you love.

awe

If you are amazed at what someone did or made, you are in **awe.**

B

Baal

One of several false gods worshipped in Bible times. He was supposed to help crops grow.

Babel

God told the people to spread out, but they came together and built the Tower of **Babel.** At **Babel,** God gave people different languages to confuse them.

A B C D E F G H I J K L M N O P Q R S T U V W X Y Z

Babylon

The capital city of the Babylonian empire. It is often used in the Bible as a symbol of people who do not follow God.

backbite

If you say bad things about someone, especially so you can hurt them, you are **backbiting.**

baker

Someone who makes bread to sell to others is a **baker.**

balm

A soothing cream used for healing or relieving pain is a **balm.** In Bible times, it was made from plants.

banner

A flag, often used in battle, so warriors can find and join others on their own side. Also used to identify a tribe or religious parade.

baptism

A way Christians show others that they follow Jesus is to be dipped in, or sprinkled with, water.

barley

A grain often used to make bread, especially by poor people.

Barnabas

A leader in the early church. He traveled with the Apostle Paul on his first trip to tell people about Jesus.

barren

If a woman is unable to have a baby, she is called **barren.** Land can also be **barren** if no crops can grow there.

basin

A wide pot or pool of water used for washing. It could also store other liquids, like oil.

bath

An amount of liquid. A **bath** was almost six gallons.

Bathsheba

One of King David's wives. David took her from another man and then had him killed. When David and **Bathsheba** had a baby, it died. They had another child, named Solomon.

beatitudes

A famous sermon by Jesus about who will be happy. You can find this sermon in chapter 5 of the book of Matthew.

befall

When something happens to a person, usually something bad. I hope something terrible does not **befall** her.

begat

To cause to happen. The father **begat** a child.

beggar

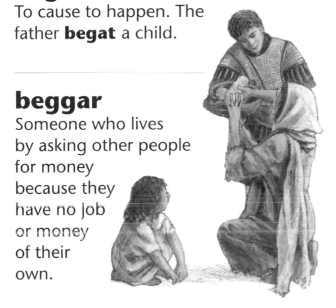

Someone who lives by asking other people for money because they have no job or money of their own.

behold

Look or consider. When John the Baptist saw Jesus, he said, "**Behold,** the Lamb of God."

believe

To trust in or be sure about. We **believe** God will keep his promises.

bell

A **bell** was not used in Bible times like a bell in a church steeple. However, a small bell was attached to the bottom of a priest's robe.

Benjamin

The youngest son of Jacob and Rachel. He was the father of one of the 12 tribes of Israel.

beryl

A precious green or yellow stone used to decorate the breastplate of the High Priest.

beseech

To strongly ask for, or beg.

beset

To attack from all sides.

besiege

To surround a city and make it surrender by cutting off the food supply.

Bethany

A city near Jerusalem where Jesus often stayed with his friends Mary and Martha and their brother Lazarus.

13

A
B
C
D
E
F
G
H
I
J
K
L
M
N
O
P
Q
R
S
T
U
V
W
X
Y
Z

Bethel

The first city in Canaan where Abraham camped and built an altar.

Bethlehem

The city where Jesus was born.

betray

To turn against a friend, especially when they need you. When Judas told the enemies of Jesus where to find Jesus, Judas **betrayed** him.

betrothed

To agree to be married. Today we say *engaged.*

Bible

The book Christians say tells us what to believe and how to live. It has two parts. The Old Testament tells the story about God and the Hebrews. The New Testament tells the story of Jesus and the early church.

bird

More than 50 kinds of birds are mentioned in the Bible, including chickens, doves, cranes, owls, hawks, and ostriches.

birthright

A gift or privilege a father gives when he dies. The first son usually received a double share.

bishop

In the New Testament, a leader in a church. The word *pastor* is often used today.

bitter herbs

Plants Hebrews eat with lamb on the Passover to remind them of their bitter, or unpleasant, years as slaves.

blessing

To wish something good for someone is to bless them. When it happens, it is a **blessing.**

blood

The red fluid that carries energy to different parts of the body. It is so important that it sometimes means "life."

blot

To wipe away. God **blots** out our sin.

body

The physical part of a person, whether they are dead or alive. The church is also called the **body** of Christ.

bond

A **bond** ties us to something or someone. It might be a rope, a chain, or a promise.

bondage

To be a slave, or to be in chains.

book

A **book** was usually written on leather or on dried and pressed plants. Then it was rolled up in a *scroll*.

Book of Life

A book in heaven where God writes the names of those who love and follow him.

booth

A shelter made of limbs and branches. The Hebrews had a special holiday where everyone lived in a **booth** for a week.

borne

Carried. A load of wood can be **borne** from the forest.

bosom

Chest or breasts, usually of someone you love. A mother holds a child in her **bosom.**

bough

A branch of a tree.

bounty

A lot of something good is a **bounty.**

bowels

The parts of a person's body that are on the inside.

branch

The part of a tree that sticks out, also called a limb. Also part of a family tree, when a child starts a new family, or **branch.**

breach

An opening made by breaking through. An enemy may **breach** a wall.

A B C D E F G H I J K L M N O P Q R S T U V W X Y Z

bride

A woman who is about to be or was just married. A father would usually choose a **bride** for his son and pay the family of the **bride** an agreed amount of money or cattle.

bridegroom

A man who is about to be, or has recently been, married.

brook

A small stream, usually one that only flows when it has been raining.

buckler

A shield used in battle. God is called our **buckler,** or protector.

bulrush

Large grasslike plant with hollow stems that grows along the riverbank.

bulwark

Towers built on the city wall. Soldiers would shoot arrows or throw rocks from the **bulwarks** to defend the city.

burden

A heavy load or weight. A **burden** could be an object or a responsibility.

butler

A high officer who did personal errands for the king. Also called a cupbearer.

C

Caesar

A title used by most Roman emperors.

Cain

He was Adam's oldest son. **Cain** killed his brother Abel. **Cain** was the first person to kill another person.

Caleb

One of the 12 spies Moses sent to check out the land of Canaan. While ten of the spies said it was too dangerous, **Caleb** and Joshua bravely said God would help them.

Calvary

The hill where Jesus died, right outside Jerusalem.

camel

A large animal used to carry people and things across the desert. A **camel** can go a long time without needing a drink of water.

Cana

The city where Jesus turned water into wine for a wedding. It was his first miracle.

Canaan

The land God promised Abraham. The Hebrews conquered and settled **Canaan** when they were freed from slavery in Egypt.

canopy

A covering made of wood or cloth, often used like a tent with no sides.

captive

A **captive** is someone who has been captured. A prisoner.

cart

A small wagon, usually with two wheels.

cedar

A kind of pine tree. **Cedars** of Lebanon were used in the temple because they were tall and straight.

centurion

An officer in the Roman army. He was in charge of 100 soldiers.

chaff

The husks and other parts of wheat or barley plants that are not eaten. **Chaff** has to be separated from the seeds before they can be used to make bread.

charity

Love, concern, or respect for people we know and for the poor.

A B C D E F G H I J K L M N O P Q R S T U V W X Y Z

chaste
Pure. It usually refers to our motives and desires.

chasten
To punish, usually to make better. A father **chastens** his children.

cheese

Milk from cows and goats was stored in bottles made from animal skins. In the heat it would turn to **cheese.**

cherub
A type of angel. Unlike most other angels, cherubim had wings. **Cherubs** were often carved into decorations in the temple.

chisel

A small tool used to cut away wood or stone.

chosen
To appoint, select, or call. The Hebrews were God's **chosen** people. In the New Testament, anyone who follows Jesus is **chosen.**

Christ

A title used to refer to Jesus. It means he was chosen for a special task, to be the Savior of the world.

chronicles
A record of what happened. The two books of **Chronicles** in the Old Testament tell the stories of kings and their accomplishments.

church
A gathering of Christians to sing, pray, and learn. May also refer to all Christians in all places and in all times.

cistern
A well or pit dug in rock or dirt to store water. **Cisterns** were important in long, dry summers.

City of David
A name for Jerusalem, where David lived when he was king. It was also a name for Bethlehem.

City of Refuge
A city people could go to if they killed someone by accident. No one could follow them there to get even.

cleave

To hold on to or cling to. You can **cleave** to a friend or to a rope.

cloven

Split. Some animals, like goats and sheep, have hooves that are **cloven.**

cock

A rooster.

coin

A **coin** is a piece of money, like a nickel or a penny. In the Bible, they had different names, like a shekel or a mite.

Colossians

The book of **Colossians** in the New Testament is a letter written by the Apostle Paul to a church in a city named Colosse.

Commandment

An important rule or law. The most famous of these are the Ten **Commandments** given to Moses by God. They were written in stone by God's own finger.

commend

You **commend** your friends when you say good things about them.

commune

To **commune** is to think about things and talk about them with others who agree with you. It also means to eat the Lord's Supper.

compassion

If you feel sad when someone else is sad or hurting, you have **compassion.** Jesus had **compassion** for people who were hungry or sick.

condemn

If you say someone has done something wrong and should be punished, you **condemn** them.

confess

When you admit you did something wrong, you **confess.**

confound

To confuse or surprise someone by doing something they do not expect.

congregation

A group of people who get together regularly to learn about God.

A B C D E F G H I J K L M N O P Q R S T U V W X Y Z

CLOTHES

Clothes in Bible times were usually made from the hair of sheep or goats, although sometimes a plant called flax was used to make linen. Most women could make and sew **clothes,** although weavers also made them and fullers dyed them different colors. **Clothing** went down to people's feet.

cloak

A square covering, worn over the shoulders. It was also used to carry things and as a blanket at night. Also called a mantle.

coat

A robe or mantle, worn over the tunic.

girdle

A belt made of cloth or leather.

headdress

Men and women wore a covering to protect their heads from the sun. Men generally wore a square piece of cloth folded into a cap. Women wore a long scarf or veil.

loincloth

Sometimes, when working, men would wrap a cloth or animal skin around their waist. This was often because they were too poor to buy other clothes.

sackcloth

When someone died, family and friends wore a coat made of rough material called **sackcloth.** They would tear it and weep to show they were sad.

sandal

These were the most common kind of shoes. Because the roads were usually dirt, you had to wash your feet when you came inside. **Sandals** were also called thongs.

tunic

Both men and women wore a long undershirt held close to the body by a girdle or belt.

veil

Women wore a long shawl. Sometimes it was decorated or had fringe. The shawl was sometimes used to cover their faces as a **veil.**

consecrate

To set something aside for a special purpose. A candle used only in the temple was **consecrated.**

contrite

To be so sorry for something you did wrong that you are sad.

Corinthians

The Apostle Paul wrote letters to Christians who lived in Corinth, a city he had visited in Greece. Two of these letters are books in the New Testament.

council

A **council** is a group of leaders who meet to talk about important things and make decisions. It can also mean the place where they meet or the meeting itself.

counsel

To suggest what to do. The suggestion is also called **counsel.**

countenance

The look on a person's face. Her **countenance** was very happy.

covenant

A **covenant** is a special promise. To show they were serious, people would eat together, give gifts, or sacrifice animals to make a **covenant.**

covet

If you want something that belongs to someone else, you **covet** it. One of the Ten Commandments says not to **covet.**

create

To make something new. God **created** the earth.

crimson

Bright red. The color of blood is **crimson.**

cross

Two pieces of wood, nailed or tied together to form an X or a T. Criminals were killed by nailing them to a **cross** to hang until they died. Jesus died on a **cross,** even though he was not a criminal.

A B C D E F G H I J K L M N O P Q R S T U V W X Y Z

crown

A band worn around the head to show someone was special. A king wore a **crown** made of gold and jewels. Jesus wore a crown of thorns.

crucify

To kill someone by nailing him or her to a cross and leaving them until they are dead. The Romans **crucified** criminals. Jesus died by **crucifixion.**

cubit

A way to measure how long something is. A **cubit** is as wide as six adult hands laid side by side, about 18 inches.

cucumber

A fruit with a thin green skin, often eaten as a vegetable.

cupbearer

A servant, usually a very important one, who tasted the king's food to make sure it had not been poisoned.

D

Daniel

A prophet who was taken to Babylon as a young man. God saved him when he was thrown in a pit with lions. He eventually became an important government leader. His story is told in the book of **Daniel.**

darkness

When there is no light, there is **darkness.**

date

A sweet fruit grown on a **date** palm. A **date** is often dried and stored for a snack.

deacon

A helper. **Deacons** were men in the early church who helped take care of others so the leaders could teach and pray.

Dead Sea

A lake in Israel that is so salty nothing can live in it, not even fish. The Jordan River flows into the **Dead Sea,** but nothing flows out of the Dead Sea.

deceit

A lie that misleads others and is hard to detect. They were tricked by **deceit.**

declare

To tell or explain clearly. A prophet **declares** the ways of God.

dedicate

To set aside or set apart for a special purpose. Both things and people can be **dedicated** to God.

deed

Something someone did. The Bible tells about good **deeds** and bad **deeds.**

deem

To view in a certain way.

deer

An animal that eats grass and leaves. Larger than a dog and very fast, **deer** were also called *hind* or *hart.*

defile

To make something so unclean or impure it can no longer be used. That candlestick is **defiled.**

defraud

To cheat someone. To **defraud** is to keep someone from getting something they need or deserve.

deliver

To rescue, free, or help escape. God is our **deliverer.**

demon

An angel who no longer follows God. The **demons'** leader is called Satan.

denarius

A **denarius** was a silver coin, roughly equal to what someone would earn for working all day.

deny

To pretend not to know or believe. Peter **denied** Jesus when Jesus was arrested.

depth
How deep something is. Usually refers to something very deep, like the ocean.

deride
To make fun of, or laugh at, in a mean way.

descendant
Someone who comes from a parent, grandparent, great grandparent, and so on, is a **descendant.**

desire
To really want something, because we long for it or take delight in it.

desolate
Lonely or deserted. A gloomy place is often **desolate.**

despair
Loss of hope. If you feel there is no possible help, you are in **despair.**

destitute
To be completely lacking what you need is to be **destitute.** Often means not having food, water, or even clothes.

Deuteronomy
A book in the Bible that retells the story of how God delivered the Hebrews from Egypt and gave them the Ten Commandments. **Deuteronomy** means "second law."

devil
A name for Satan, the chief of all angels who no longer follow God.

dew
The wetness on plants and grass early in the morning.

diadem
A crown, used mostly by kings and queens as a symbol of their power.

discern
To tell the good from the bad is to **discern** the difference, even if it is not obvious.

disciple
A follower or student. Jesus' closest followers were called **disciples.**

disperse
To scatter or spread around is to **disperse.**

divorce
To end a marriage.

doctrine
Doctrine is what a group of Christians believes and teaches about God, humans, Jesus, sin, and other issues.

donkey

A horselike animal used to carry heavy loads. **Donkeys** were valuable because they could live in areas that were dry.

doorkeeper
Someone who guards a door or opens it for others. Not usually a soldier.

doorposts
The wood or stone around a door that holds it in place.

doubt
If you are not sure something is true, you **doubt** it.

dove

A bird similar to a pigeon. **Doves** are gentle and loyal. Noah sent out a **dove** to learn when the flood was over.

dowry
A gift that was given to a bride's father by her husband's family. A large **dowry** meant the bride's family was wealthy.

drachma
A coin worth a day's pay, similar to the Roman denarius.

draw
To take water from a well or a spring.

dread
A feeling that something bad is going to happen.

dream
A picture in your mind while you are sleeping. The dreams of priests and kings sometimes brought messages from God.

A B C D E F G H I J K L M N O P Q R S T U V W X Y Z

drunk

When a person drinks too much wine. When people are **drunk,** they do not think or act like they do when they are not **drunk.**

dumb

Being unable to speak. **Dumb** does not mean stupid or unable to learn.

dung

The waste from animals or humans. **Dung** could be used to help make plants grow or burned as fuel when dried.

dust

Loose dirt. God made Adam from **dust.**

dwell

The place you live or stay. People **dwell** in a house.

dye

Dye is used to make clothes a different color. It is made from parts of plants or animals.

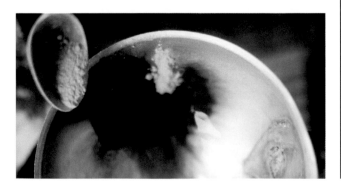

eagle

A large bird that eats small animals.

earnest

A pledge or promise, often made with a payment of money.

east wind

A dry, hot wind that blows out of the desert.

Ecclesiastes

A book in the Old Testament. Its message is that life has no real purpose without God.

edict

An official order or command.

edify

To **edify** is to encourage someone to do the right thing.

Egypt

A land in northern Africa. The ruler was called pharaoh. The Hebrews were slaves in **Egypt** before God helped them escape. The Nile River flows through **Egypt.**

elder

An older member of a family, tribe, or church.

elephant

The largest animal, other than a whale. **Elephants** were used to carry or move heavy things.

Eli

A judge and high priest who trained Samuel when he was a boy. Samuel grew up to be a prophet.

Elijah

A famous prophet who took a stand against priests and kings who did not follow God. **Elijah** once called down fire from heaven. He was taken up to heaven in a whirlwind.

Elisha

A prophet who helped Elijah and later took his place.

Emmanuel

A name that means "God with us." Jesus was called **Emmanuel.**

entice

To attract someone by offering something he or she wants.

entreat

To ask in a serious way. She **entreated** him to go to the temple.

envy

When you want something that belongs to someone else, you **envy** it. The Ten Commandments tell us not to **envy.**

Ephesians

A book in the New Testament. It is a letter the Apostle Paul wrote to Christians living in Ephesus.

ephod

A special vest worn by the high priest. It had gold thread and jewels.

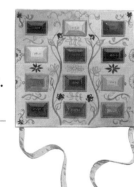

epistle

A letter. The Apostle Paul wrote many **epistles,** 13 of which are now books in the New Testament.

A B C D E F G H I J K L M N O P Q R S T U V W X Y Z

esteem

If you think something is important and valuable, you **esteem** it.

eternal

If something is **eternal,** it lasts forever.

eunuch

A male servant who served the king's family.

Eve

The first woman and the mother of everyone. God made **Eve** from Adam's rib.

evil

Anything that is bad or wrong because it opposes God is **evil.**

ewe

A female sheep is a **ewe.**

exalt

To lift or raise up an idea or person as good or great. We **exalt** God.

exhort

To warn or encourage someone to act in a certain way. We **exhort** each other to do right.

exile

To **exile** is to send away. When people are sent away from their homes, they are exiled.

Exodus

A book in the Old Testament. It tells how the Israelites escaped from Egypt, where they were slaves.

extol

To tell others how good or great something or someone is. We **extol** the glory of God.

Ezekiel

A prophet who warned the Hebrews that Jerusalem would be destroyed. In the book of **Ezekiel,** he promised God's kingdom would come again.

Ezra

When the Israelites came back to Jerusalem from Babylon, **Ezra** taught them to pray and read the scriptures again.

F

faint

If you are very tired or weak, you are **faint.**

faith

Believing and trusting. We have **faith** in God and his promises.

falcon

A bird that hunts small animals. People often train these birds.

famine

When there is no food, there is a **famine.** This happens when crops do not grow or because an enemy does not let food into a city.

fare

When things go well, they **fare** well. How do you **fare** today?

farmer

A person who lives by raising crops or cattle, both to use and to sell, is a **farmer.**

fast

To go without food on purpose, usually so you can pray.

fathom

The width of an adult's arms stretched out. The water was two **fathoms** deep.

favor

Approval or kindness. Esther was **favored** by the king.

fear

In Bible times, **fear** often referred to honor or respect. To **fear** God did not mean to be afraid of him.

feast

A big, delicious meal shared with many guests. Sometimes a **feast** lasted all day.

A B C D E F G H I J K L M N O P Q R S T U V W X Y Z

fellowship

When we spend time with people we agree with, we have **fellowship** with them.

fetter

A chain, used to keep prisoners from getting away.

firmament

The sky, including the stars. God made the **firmament.**

firstfruits

When the people of Israel harvested their crops or counted their baby animals, they gave the first and best to God. They brought the **firstfruits** to the priests.

fisher, fisherman

Someone who catches fish to eat and sell.

Fish Gate

A gate in the wall around Jerusalem where fishermen brought their catch to sell.

flatter

When you **flatter** people, you say nice things to them so they will like you or do what you want.

flood

A **flood** is when it rains so hard the rivers get full and flow out over the land. Once God sent a great **flood** to destroy the earth.

fold

A fenced place to hold in animals. Shepherds keep their sheep in a **fold** overnight.

follow

To come after. The disciples **followed** Jesus.

folly

Something silly or foolish is **folly.**

FOOD

Meals were simple, and usually eaten only twice a day—near noon and later in the evening. **Food** was cooked over a fire in a small hole in the dirt floor called a hearth. Bread was prepared in ovens made of stone or dirt.

bread

This was made by grinding wheat or barley between two stones and mixing it with salt, yeast, olive oil, and milk or water. Then it was baked in or near a fire.

fowl

Birds that were eaten. Chicken, duck, geese, and turkey are kinds of **fowl.**

fruit

Figs were eaten right off the tree or made into cakes that could be saved for later. Other **fruits** included apples and melons.

grapes

Grapes were very important, since the juice could be made into wine and kept for later.

meat

The Hebrews ate beef, goats, and sheep, especially lamb. They were not allowed to eat camel, rabbit, pork, or shrimp.

milk

Milk from cows and goats was stored in bottles made from animal skins. In the heat, it would turn to cheese.

nuts

Almonds and dates were popular. Dates grew on palm trees.

pottage

A thick soup or stew, often made with lentils and meat.

salt

Salt was used to season food. It was so valuable that it was sometimes used for money.

vegetables

Onions were widely used because they were easy to store and keep. Garlic, leeks, and cucumbers were also popular.

forbear
To wait for someone or something to change.

forbid
If you tell someone not to do something, you **forbid** it. God **forbids** telling lies.

ford
A shallow place in a river where people and animals can cross.

forgive
To excuse someone for something he or she did wrong. Jesus **forgives** our sins.

forsake
To let go or give up. Jesus will not **forsake** us.

fortress
A safe place, like an army fort with strong walls.

foundation
The flat, stone base of a building is its **foundation**.

fountain
A place where water springs up out of the ground.

frankincense
A perfume made from the sap of a tree.

fruit
Food that grows on trees. We wait to pick the **fruit** until it is ripe. Also used to describe children or the good things we do.

fuller
A **fuller** is a person who makes or washes clothes.

furnace
An oven that is used to bake bricks, bread, or pottery. It is very hot inside a **furnace**.

fury
Very strong anger is **fury**.

Gabriel
The name of an angel who often brought important messages from God.

Galatians
A book in the New Testament. It was a letter from the Apostle Paul to people who lived in a town called Galatia.

Galilee
A part of northern Israel where Jesus grew up. Also the name of a large lake.

gall
Any bitter thing. The word comes from a poisonous plant.

garden
A place to grow plants. Jesus went to a **garden** to pray.

garment
The clothes you wear are your **garments.**

gate
Used in the Bible for any door to a house, garden, fold, or city.

generation
People who had the same parents and grandparents. Also people who lived at the same time in history.

Genesis
Genesis is the beginning of something. The first book in the Bible is called **Genesis.**

gentile
People who are not descendants of Abraham are called **gentiles.**

Gethsemane

A garden where Jesus prayed before he was killed.

giant

People who were strong and very tall were called **giants.**

Gideon

A judge in Israel who once defeated a very large army with only 300 soldiers. God helped **Gideon.**

gird

To put on a belt or to fasten with a belt.

glean

To gather. Poor people were allowed to **glean** grain or grapes after the field had been harvested so they would not go hungry.

glory

The brightness of God is very great. We refer to it as his **glory.** When we talk or think about how great he is, we **glorify** him.

glutton

Someone who eats too much over and over again is called a **glutton.**

gnash

If you grind your teeth together when you are very angry or upset, you **gnash** your teeth.

goat

An animal similar to a sheep. **Goat** milk was used to drink or make cheese. **Goat** hair was used to make clothes.

God

God has no beginning and no end. He created everything and everyone.

gold

A precious yellow metal used for money and jewelry.

Golgotha

A hill that looked something like a skull. Jesus was crucified on **Golgotha.** It is also called Calvary.

Goliath

A giant killed by King David when he was still a young boy.

good

That which is pleasant and enjoyable. Anything **good** is like God or comes from God.

gospel

Good news. The first four books of the New Testament are called the **gospels** because they tell the good news that Jesus died for our sins.

gourd

A fruit with a hard shell. **Gourds** were often emptied and dried to use as cups.

governor

An officer who ruled over a smaller area for the king or emperor.

grace

A gift or a favor that does not depend on what we have done. God's **grace** is a result of his love.

grant

To give or allow. The king may **grant** you a special favor.

grave

When people die, they are buried in a **grave.** In Bible times, this was sometimes a cave.

Greek

The language of people from Greece. Much of the New Testament was written in **Greek.**

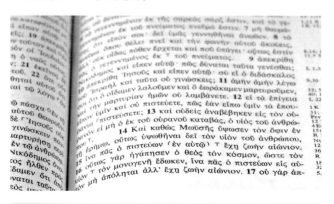

guard

To watch over or protect something is to **guard** it. The person who does this is also called a **guard.**

H

guilt

If you feel bad when you do something wrong, you feel **guilt.** Even if you do not feel bad but you did something wrong, you are **guilty.**

Habakkuk

A book in the Old Testament, written by a prophet named **Habakkuk.** God told him that wicked people would be destroyed.

hades

A place for the dead, sometimes known as hell.

Hagar

A servant of Sarah, Abraham's wife. **Hagar** had a son named Ishmael.

Haggai

When the people of Israel returned from Babylon, the prophet **Haggai** encouraged them to finish rebuilding the temple.

hail

A greeting, like hello. It means "Rejoice! Be glad!"

hallelujah

A word used in worship. It means "praise the Lord."

hallowed

Set apart as something special. Jesus said God's name was **hallowed.**

handmaid

A servant girl. Mary, the mother of Jesus, said she was God's **handmaid.**

hare

A rabbit.

hart

Another name for a deer.

haste

Speed. If you do something quickly, you do it **hastily.**

heal

To make well. Jesus often **healed** the sick.

heap

To pile up or add. The man **heaped** stones together to make an altar.

heart

Hebrews believed the **heart** was where we think or decide. We would say mind or brain.

hearth

A hole in the ground inside a house or tent. A fire was built in the **hearth** for cooking or heating.

heathen

Someone who does not know or follow the true God is called a **heathen.**

heaven

A place of perfect happiness. God's throne is in **heaven.**

Hebrew

A descendant of Abraham, also called an Israelite or Jew. Most of the Old Testament was written in the **Hebrew** language. **Hebrews** is also a book in the New Testament.

heed

To pay close attention.

heifer

A young cow, older than a calf.

hence

From this place or after this time. Let us go **hence.**

herald

An officer who carried a king's message.

herb

Any grass or green plant was called an **herb.**

heritage
Something we get from our parents or ancestors. It can be physical, like a house or field. It may also be a habit, tradition, or attitude.

Herod
The title of Roman governors in Israel. Three different **Herods** ruled during the life of Jesus.

hew
To cut with blows from an axe or chisel. You **hew** logs into firewood or stone into blocks.

high priest
The chief priest of the Israelites. Aaron was the first **high priest.**

hin
A gallon.

hinder
The back of something was its **hinder** part. Can also mean to keep back or delay. He **hindered** her from making bread.

holy
Completely free of evil. God is **holy.** Things set aside for him are also **holy.**

Holy Place
A room in the temple. No one could enter the **Holy Place** except the high priest.

homer
An amount of flour. It was about six big baskets full.

honor
To **honor** is to show how great something is by what we say and do.

hope
Expecting someone to keep a promise. We **hope** in God.

hornet
A kind of yellow and black stinging insect.

horse
Horses were used in battle because they were faster than mules or camels.

HOUSEHOLD OBJECTS

Some **household objects** in Bible times were similar to those we use today, but many were very different from what we have in our houses.

basket

A **basket** is like a bowl made out of straw. People used baskets to carry or store their things.

bed

In most homes, a **bed** was a straw mat, rolled out on the floor.

bench

People often sat on the ground, but sometimes they had a **bench** made of wood or stone.

candlestick

A **candlestick** holds a candle, sometimes several of them.

cup

A **cup** in the Bible was made from clay, wood, or even gold.

kitchen

The **kitchen** was usually outside the home so smoke from the fire would not fill the house. Dishes and pots were very simple. Most homes had just a few wooden spoons, scrapers, or hooks.

lamp

A **lamp** was usually a small pot made of clay with a wick like a candle. It burned olive oil, not wax.

pitcher

A **pitcher** was made of clay, and it was used to hold or pour water or wine. They were also called **vessels.**

table

The **table** in a house was very low. People would often lie on their sides on the floor beside the **table** to eat or visit.

wineskin

A **wineskin** was a container for holding wine. The **wineskin** was made from animal skins.

hosanna
A prayer. It means "save us!"

Hosea
A prophet in the Old Testament who reminded the Jews that God loved them. He wrote the book of **Hosea.**

hospitality
Welcoming others, especially strangers.

host
One who welcomes others is a **host.** It also means a large group of people or angels.

housetop
People used the top of their houses like a porch, where they worked outside or rested.

humble
If we care more about God and others than about ourselves, we are **humble.**

hymn
A song we sing to God. It is usually a song about how great God is.

hypocrite
A person who pretends to believe something he does not actually believe is a **hypocrite.**

hyssop
A small, bushy plant used in worship and healing.

I

idle
Lazy. A person who does not work is **idle.**

idol
A false god, sometimes represented by a doll or statue. To worship a false god is **idolatry.**

immortality
Not able to die. Someone who will never die is **immortal.**

impart
To give. The teacher will **impart** a lesson.

impute

To give credit or blame to someone else.

incarnation

When God became a man named Jesus, we say he was **incarnated,** or given a body.

incense

Perfume burned to give a sweet smell.

indignation

Anger, especially when you think you or someone else was treated badly.

infirmity

A weakness or sickness. His broken bone was an **infirmity.**

inhabitant

Someone who lives in a place. She was an **inhabitant** of the city.

inherit

To receive property and money when someone dies. This gift is called an **inheritance.**

Isaac

The only son of Abraham and his wife, Sarah. His name means "laughter."

Isaiah

A famous prophet who told people a "suffering servant" would come. He wrote the book of **Isaiah** in the Old Testament.

Ishmael

Abraham's first son. His mother, Hagar, was a servant of Abraham's wife, Sarah.

Israel

Abraham's grandson was named Jacob, but God changed it to **Israel.** The nation that came from Abraham was also called **Israel.**

A B C D E F G H I J K L M N O P Q R S T U V W X Y Z

Jacob

A son of Isaac and Rebekah. Later God changed his name to Israel. **Jacob** had 12 sons, whose children became the 12 tribes of Israel.

Jacob's ladder

Jacob had a dream about a ladder that went up to heaven.

Jacob's well

A well Jacob dug that was still being used when Jesus lived, thousands of years later.

James

Two of the disciples who followed Jesus were named **James.** Jesus also had a half-brother named **James** who may have written the book of **James** in the New Testament.

Jehosaphat

A king in Judah who tried to end the worship of false gods and teach the people the law of God.

Jeremiah

An important Old Testament prophet who warned people to follow God or be punished. The book of **Jeremiah** was written by his secretary, Baruch.

Jericho

A city destroyed by the Hebrews when God made the walls fall down.

Jerusalem

The city where King David ruled Israel. The temple was also there.

Jesse

The father of King David.

Jesus

The Son of God. His mother, Mary, was a descendant of King David. **Jesus'** name means "one who saves us."

NAMES OF JESUS

In the Bible, there are more than 200 **names** and titles for Jesus. Here are some of the **names** he gave himself in the New Testament. He said "I am the" . . .

Bread of Life

Jesus said there was something more important than food. Just like we might be hungry for food, we should be hungry for God.

Gate for the Sheep

We are like sheep, and Jesus is the "gate" we go through to get to God.

Good Shepherd

Jesus cares for us, just as a shepherd cares for his sheep.

Light of the World

Jesus wants us to see things the way they really are. He is the "light" that helps us see what God wants.

Resurrection and the Life

Since Jesus would die and then live again, he promised that we could do the same.

True Vine

Jesus said he is the vine and we are the branches. We can produce fruit, like grapes on a vine, but the fruit would be love, joy, and peace.

Way, the Truth, and the Life

When Jesus said this, he was putting several of these ideas together. He is the gate and the light for us to live with him in heaven.

A B C D E F G H I J K L M N O P Q R S T U V W X Y Z

Jew

At first this name was used for people from the tribe of Judah, but it now refers to all those descended from Abraham, Isaac, and Jacob.

Joab

A nephew of King David who commanded the army.

Joash

The name of two different kings, one in Judah and one in Israel.

Job

A patient man whose troubles are told in a book of poetry called **Job.** This book is in the Old Testament.

Joel

A prophet with this name wrote the book of **Joel** and promised that God's spirit would come.

John

A fisher who became one of Jesus' closest disciples. He wrote books that are in the New Testament.

John the Baptist

A prophet who baptized Jesus. He was Jesus' cousin.

Jonah

A prophet who was swallowed by a big fish when he would not do what God said. Later the fish spit him out, and he did what God told him to do. His story is told in the book of **Jonah**.

Jordan

A river the Hebrews had to cross when they entered the Promised Land. Jesus was later baptized in the **Jordan** River. Today, **Jordan** is a country on the east bank of the River **Jordan.**

Joseph

A son of Jacob. He became a ruler in Egypt and helped save the Hebrews when there was no food. **Joseph** was also the name of Jesus' earthly father, who was married to his mother, Mary.

Joshua

A leader of Israel who took over when Moses died. He was a great soldier who led them when they entered the Promised Land.

Jubilee

A celebration held every 50 years. No crops were planted so the land could rest and all slaves were freed.

Judah

A son of Jacob and a tribe in Israel. Later, when the kingdom divided, the southern kingdom was called **Judah.**

Judas

A disciple who turned Jesus over to be crucified. A different Judas was the half-brother of Jesus and wrote the book of **Jude.**

Judea

Another name for Judah, the southern kingdom.

judge

A person chosen to explain the law.

Judges

Before there were kings in Israel, people were led by **judges.** This story is told in the Old Testament book of **Judges.**

judgment

A decision, usually about what is right and what is wrong.

just

If something is **just,** it is fair and right.

justice

Doing what is fair and right.

justified

To be made right. Usually this means to have a right relationship with God.

K

kin
A family member or relative.

kindle
To start a fire.

kine
Cows.

king
The ruler of a nation. In the Bible, the **king** led the army. A **king** often inherits his position and rules for life.

kingdom
The land ruled by a king. God rules everything, and people who follow him are part of the **Kingdom** of God.

Kings
The name of two books in the Bible that tell the story of Israel's kings.

kneel
To get down on your knees, usually to show respect. We **kneel** in worship and sometimes people **kneel** before a king.

knit
To join or tie together.

know
To understand very well.

GOOD KING, BAD KING

More than 40 **kings** ruled the Hebrews. Some of the **kings** followed God and some did not. Here a few examples:

GOOD KINGS

David

A shepherd boy who became king, **David** was a warrior and a songwriter who loved God and made the nation larger and safer.

Solomon

David's son **Solomon** was very wise and built a beautiful temple for worshipping God.

Uzziah

Uzziah worshipped God and restored the power of the kingdom. He rebuilt the walls around Jerusalem.

Hezekiah

After his father Ahaz quit following God, **Hezekiah** destroyed the idols and started worshipping God in the temple again.

Josiah

Josiah became king when he was 8 years old. He loved God and repaired the temple that had fallen down. He also had the Bible read out loud to the people.

BAD KINGS

Ahab

Ahab added more idols beside the golden calf. His evil wife, Jezebel, had many priests killed. The prophet Elijah opposed **Ahab** and Jezebel.

Ahaziah

After Athaliah's husband died, she had members of her own family killed so no one could rule except her son **Ahaziah.** Athaliah was the daughter of Jezebel.

Jehoiakim

Jehoiakim charged the people very high taxes and worshipped idols. He tried to kill the prophet Jeremiah.

Jeroboam

Jeroboam made the people worship an idol of a golden calf. He was so bad the Bible says 15 other bad kings were "like Jeroboam."

Manassah

Manassah rebuilt places to worship idols that his father, Hezekiah, had destroyed. He murdered many people, including his own sons.

L

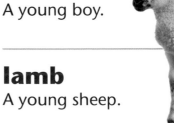

lad
A young boy.

lamb
A young sheep.

lame
When your legs don't work well. When you are **lame,** you cannot walk or you limp when you do.

lament
To express deep sorrow, usually with words or sounds.

Lamentations
The prophet Jeremiah wrote the book of **Lamentations.** It was about his sorrow when the people did not follow God.

languish

To become weak or fade away.

laver

A large bowl, used in the temple to wash people and things used in worship.

Law

Rules and teachings about what is right. **Law** also refers to all or part of the Old Testament because it contains many of God's **laws.**

lawful

Allowed by law. What she did was **lawful.**

Lazarus

The brother of Mary and Martha and a friend of Jesus. When he died, Jesus brought him back to life.

leather

Cloth or coverings made from animal skin.

leaven

Something in bread that makes it lighter and fluffier. Also called yeast.

legion

A group of Roman soldiers, between 3,000 and 6,000 men. A **legion** can also mean any very large number.

lentils

A seed often used to make soup or stew. Similar to a dried pea.

A B C D E F G H I J K L M N O P Q R S T U V W X Y Z

leopard
A large, wild cat. A **leopard** is smaller than a lion.

leper
Leprosy is a terrible skin disease. Someone who had the disease was called a **leper.**

lest
For fear that. Be careful, **lest** you get hurt.

Levi
Levi was one of Jacob's 12 sons and head of one of the 12 tribes of Israel. His tribe took care of the temple. A disciple of Jesus named Matthew was also called **Levi.**

levy
When the king forced people to be in the army or help build a road or building, it was called a **levy.**

liberty
Being free to choose or do what you want.

lie
To say something that is not true.

light
Not dark. Often means that which is true and good. God is **light.**

lily
A flowering plant. A **lily** has a star-shaped flower with six petals.

lintel
The stone or wood support above a door.

lion
A wild cat known for its strength and size. Jesus is known as the **Lion** of Judah.

loathe
To dislike something so much you will not have anything to do with it.

locust
An insect. **Locusts** are hungry all the time. In groups, they can eat and destroy all the plants in an entire field.

A B C D E F G H I J K L M N O P Q R S T U V W X Y Z

lodge
To spend the night somewhere. We will **lodge** in Galilee.

Lord
Master or sir. A title for God.

Lord's Prayer
A prayer Jesus used as an example when his disciples asked him how to pray.

Lord's Supper
The night before he died, Jesus had supper with his disciples. He asked them to remember him by having bread and wine together. This is called Communion in many churches.

Lot
Abraham's nephew. When God destroyed the city of Sodom, he saved **Lot.**

lots
Similar to dice, **lots** were stones used to decide what to do.

love
A deep desire for another person's safety and success. God is the best example of **love.**

lowly
Humble. More concerned about what other people want or need than about what we want or need.

Lucifer
An important angel who decided not to follow God and got other angels to follow him. Also called Satan or the devil.

Luke
Luke was a doctor and a friend of the Apostle Paul. He wrote two books in the New Testament—**Luke** and Acts.

M

magi

Wise men, usually teachers and scientists. Several **magi** brought gifts to Jesus when he was a baby.

magistrate

Another word for judge or ruler.

magnify

To praise highly, telling how great someone is. We **magnify** God.

maimed

Someone who lost an arm or leg is **maimed.** This could happen in a battle or an accident.

maker

Someone who creates something. God is our **maker.**

Malachi

Old Testament prophet who wrote the book of **Malachi.** He questioned the priest and people about why they did not follow God.

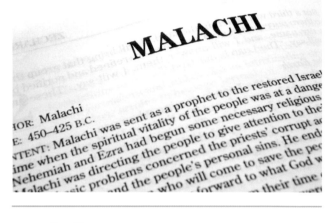

malefactor

Someone who does evil. Usually someone who does not obey the law and hurts others.

malice

A desire or plan to hurt someone.

manger

A box for feeding hay to cows and other animals.

manifold

Many. God has given us **manifold** gifts.

mantle

A cloak or robe worn over other clothes.

Mark

Mark is the second book in the New Testament. It was written by **Mark,** a friend of the Apostle Paul.

marriage

When a man and woman promise to spend their lives together. Jesus taught that **marriage** was created by God.

marrow

The soft part inside a bone. In the Bible, **marrow** sometimes means the best part.

Mary Magdalene

Mary Magdalene was a friend and follower of Jesus. She was healed by him.

mason

A **mason** works with bricks and stones to build walls.

master

A leader or teacher. People often called Jesus **Master.**

Matthew

The first book in the New Testament. It was written by **Matthew,** one of the 12 disciples.

Matthias

Matthias replaced Judas as one of the 12 disciples.

measure

A certain amount of liquid or dry products, usually food. Can also be the way this amount is determined.

A B C D E F G H I J K L M N O P Q R S T U V W X Y Z

MIRACLES IN THE BIBLE

When something happens only God could do, it is a **miracle.** Here are just a few of these stories:

Daniel

▲ Survived after being thrown in a pit with hungry lions

▲ Read God's handwriting on a wall during a large party for a king

Elijah

▲ Kept the rain away for over three years so people would begin to pray
▲ Called fire down on an altar, even after he poured buckets of water over it

▲ Fed a widow for many days with a handful of flour, and then raised her son from the dead

Jesus

▲ Turned water into wine at a wedding party
▲ Fed 5,000 people with 5 small loaves of bread and 2 fishes

- ▲ Walked on water and calmed a storm
- ▲ Healed many people who were blind, crippled, or had other diseases
- ▲ Brought Lazarus back to life after he had been dead for several days

- ▲ Came back from the dead himself

Moses

- ▲ Held out his staff to cause the Red Sea to part so the people could escape

- ▲ Struck a rock with his staff so water flowed out for thousands of Hebrews
- ▲ Told the people God would (and did) send bread from heaven, called *manna*

A B C D E F G H I J K L M N O P Q R S T U V W X Y Z

mediator

Someone who goes between two other people or groups to help them agree. The **mediator** helps them solve a problem.

meditate

To think about something carefully and quietly.

meek

Gentle and humble. People who are **meek** are not pushy or loud.

melody

To make a **melody** meant to play a song on a harp or other musical instrument.

mercy

Showing kindness to others who are hurting or weak. God has **mercy** for his people.

mercy seat

The top of the Ark of the Covenant, which was covered with gold. God met the high priest at the **mercy seat.**

merry

Happy and carefree. The people at the party were **merry.**

Messiah

The one chosen by God to save and lead everyone in the world. Jesus is the **Messiah.**

Micah

A book in the Old Testament written by the prophet **Micah.** He was concerned about how rich people treat poor people.

Michael

A chief angel, or archangel, who looked out for the Hebrews.

Midian

One of the sons of Abraham, although his descendants, the **Midianites,** were often enemies of the Hebrews.

midwife
A woman who helps other women have their babies.

mill
A place where wheat or barley is ground into flour by large stones, called millstones.

minister
To serve. We should **minister** to people who have needs.

miracle
When something happens only God could do, it is a **miracle.** The first **miracle** Jesus did was turning water into wine.

mire
Thick mud. They got stuck in the **mire.**

mirth
Mirth is when people are joyful and glad. She was filled with **mirth.**

mistress
A woman who owns or takes care of a house.

Moab
A grandson of Abraham whose people became a nation near Israel. The people were called **Moabites.**

mock
To **mock** someone is to make fun of them and say mean things about them.

money
In the Old Testament, people often traded their things for other things they needed. In the New Testament, they used coins for **money.**

moneychanger
In the temple, you could only use Hebrew money. If you had Greek or Roman money, the **moneychangers** would trade it for Hebrew coins.

MUSICAL INSTRUMENTS

The Hebrews had many **musical instruments.** Some were used only in the temple, while others were used every day.

cymbals

Flat pieces of metal clashed together, usually to start a choir or a parade.

dulcimer

Also called a harp, this was played by striking the strings with small, soft hammers.

harp

A musical instrument with strings. A variety of instruments were called **harps.**

lute

A kind of harp. It probably had ten strings.

lyre

A small harp. It had a box along the bottom to make the sound louder.

pipe

You blow into it, like a flute. It was made from a hollow reed with holes punched in it.

shofar

Made from a ram's horn, the **shofar** only made two or three sounds. It was used to call people together for a meeting or gather soldiers in battle.

tambourine

A small handheld drum. The **tambourine** was often used to make noise at parties or other celebrations.

timbrel

A kind of rattle, with loose rings and bells attached to a small wooden frame. A **timbrel** sounded something like a tambourine.

trumpet

This was long and straight. Also simply called a horn.

month

Months were one or two days shorter in Bible times than they are now. Each **month** began on the new moon.

Moses

The leader God chose to lead the Hebrews out of slavery in Egypt. God gave **Moses** the Ten Commandments.

Mount of Olives

A low mountain outside of Jerusalem where Jesus prayed before he was crucified.

mourn

To be sad, especially when someone dies. You can **mourn** any time you lose something important to you.

mouse

Almost any small, furry creature like a hamster, mouse, or rat was called a **mouse.**

multitude

A large crowd is called a **multitude.**

mute

Someone who is unable to speak is called a **mute.**

muzzle

A leather or wire covering for the mouth of an animal to keep it from eating or biting. They put a **muzzle** on the donkey.

myrrh

A gummy substance collected from a tree that was used to make oil and perfume. The magi brought **myrrh** to the baby Jesus.

myrtle

A kind of small tree with good smelling leaves and white flowers.

mystery

Something hard to understand is a **mystery.** Sometimes the meaning is invisible or hidden.

A B C D E F G H I J K L M N O P Q R S T U V W X Y Z

Nahum

A book in the Old Testament written by the prophet **Nahum.** He said God would destroy Assyria.

Nathan

A prophet in the time of King David and King Solomon. He said David would not be the one to build the temple in Jerusalem.

Nazareth

A town where Jesus lived when he was a boy. Jesus was from **Nazareth.**

Nazarite

A person who made a special promise to serve God and separate himself from others. John the Baptist was a **Nazarite.**

Nebuchadnezzar

A king of Babylon who captured Jerusalem and took many of its people back to Babylon.

Nehemiah

A Hebrew who served the king of Persia and was allowed to rebuild the walls of Jerusalem. His story is told in the Old Testament book of **Nehemiah.**

New Testament

The books of the Bible that tell the story of Jesus and the early church.

Nile

A large river in Egypt.

Nineveh

The capital of Assyria. **Nineveh** turned to God after the prophet Jonah preached to them.

Noah

Noah obeyed God by building a large boat, called an ark, to save his family from a huge flood.

Numbers

A book in the Old Testament that lists the names of the first Hebrew tribes and families.

numbers

Characters used for counting, such as 1, 2, 3. Greeks, Romans, Egyptians, and Hebrews all had their own **numbers.**

Obadiah

An Old Testament book made up of sermons by the prophet **Obadiah.**

obey

To hear and do what we are told to do. We should **obey** God.

observe

To watch, keep, or practice. Hebrews **observe** the Sabbath.

occupy

To settle in a place. The Israelites **occupied** Canaan.

odor

A smell. Some pleasing **odors** were used in temple worship.

A B C D E F G H I J K L M N O P Q R S T U V W X Y Z

A B C D E F G H I J K L M N O P Q R S T U V W X Y Z

offense
Breaking a rule or law. An **offense** can also mean to cause to stumble, as in causing someone else to break the rule.

offering
A gift or sacrifice, usually in worship. The people brought **offerings** to the Lord.

office
A position or title. He held a high **office**.

offspring
Children and grandchildren. **Offspring** are also called descendants.

oil
Oil was usually made from olives. It was used for medicine and food. It was also used for fuel in lamps.

ointment
A sweet-smelling oil used on special occasions, including funerals.

Old Testament
The books in the Bible written before Jesus was born. These books tell the story of the Hebrew people.

olive
The fruit from an **olive** tree. **Olives** were pressed to make oil for food and lamplight.

omega
The last letter of the Greek alphabet.

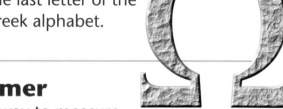

omer
A way to measure grain. An **omer** is about the size of a half gallon.

onion
A common vegetable, widely used because it is easy to store.

onyx
A shiny stone used for jewelry.

oppress
To take advantage of someone who is weaker than you are.

oracle

Words or messages from God. The person who brings this message is also called an **oracle.**

ordain

To appoint or set aside for a special service. A pastor or minister is **ordained.**

order

To arrange or organize the right way. Everything must be in **order.**

ordinance

A law. God gave the Hebrews many **ordinances.**

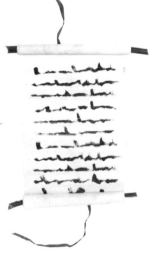

outcast

People who are driven from their homes by war or an order from the king are **outcasts.**

overcome

To win. If one army defeats another army, they **overcome** them.

overflow

To spill or flood. The river **overflows** in the rainy season.

overlaid

Covered. The box was **overlaid** with silver.

overseer

The person in charge. The **overseer** looked out for the king's interests.

owl

A bird. **Owls** hunt mice and small creatures, mostly at night.

ox

In the Bible, this refers to a cow. Cows, or **oxen,** were used as food as well as for carrying or pulling things.

P

palace

The home of a king or high priest. A **palace** is a nice home, with strong walls and beautiful furniture.

Palestine

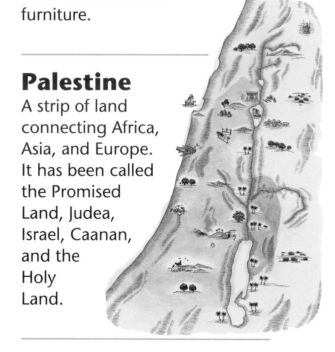

A strip of land connecting Africa, Asia, and Europe. It has been called the Promised Land, Judea, Israel, Caanan, and the Holy Land.

palm

The **palm** tree referred to in the Bible grows near the Jordan River and has a seed with a soft shell, called a date.

Palm Sunday

On the Sunday before he was crucified, some people took branches from palm trees and waved them around Jesus, calling him the King.

palsy

A sickness where people cannot move their arms or legs. Jesus healed a man with **palsy.**

pangs

Sharp pains.

papyrus

A plant that grows near the water. It has tall, hollow stems and was used to make paper.

parable

A short, simple story used to explain an important idea. Jesus told many **parables.**

paradise

A beautiful park or garden. **Paradise** is used to describe the garden where God made Adam and Eve and the place Christians go when they die.

parchment

A kind of paper made from animal skins.

pardon

To forgive and not punish. God will **pardon** our sins.

partake

To join in. He decided to **partake** of the meal.

paschal

Refers to a Hebrew festival called Passover. The family ate the **paschal** lamb.

passage

A place to cross a river. Also the right to travel. They were looking for safe **passage.**

passion

Pain or suffering. Christians think of the **passion** of Christ on the cross.

Passover

A feast when Hebrews remember that God brought them out of slavery in Egypt. That night many Egyptians died, but God passed over the Hebrews.

pastor

A shepherd. This word is also used to describe one who cares for people in a church.

A B C D E F G H I J K L M N O P Q R S T U V W X Y Z

PARABLES OF JESUS

Jesus often used short stories to explain what he meant. These stories are called **parables.**

Good Samaritan

Many Hebrews did not like people from Samaria, but Jesus told a story about how one of them helped a man who had been robbed and beaten. The one who actually helps us is our neighbor, he said.

Mustard Seed

Jesus said a mustard seed was very little but a tree still grew from it. You only need a little faith for something big to happen.

Prodigal Son

A young man took his share of his father's money and went off to be with his friends and spend the money on foolish things. When he was broke and poor, he came back to his father, who still loved him and threw a big party to celebrate. God is always happy when his children return, Jesus said.

Rich Fool

Jesus told a story about a man who counted all his money and his crops and was full of pride. Jesus said our treasure should not be things we can see but things we cannot see.

Sheep from the Goats

Jesus talked about separating the wheat from the weeds and the sheep from the goats. Even though we cannot always tell the difference, when God comes he will know which is which. He knows who believes in him and who does not.

Sower

A farmer went out to plant some seed. Some seed fell on good soil and grew. Other seed fell on bad soil and did not grow. Jesus said the seed was like the Word of God—not everyone believes or understands it.

Treasure in a Field

If you knew a treasure was hidden in a field, you would go buy the field. You would also look hard for a lost pearl or coin. Jesus said God was a treasure, and we should try very hard to find him.

Wedding Banquet

A king had a big dinner when his son got married, but many people he invited did not come. So the king invited everyone. He still expected them to dress for a wedding, however, and he had one man thrown out of the party who came in his work clothes. God invites everyone to his dinner, too, but he expects them to prepare the right way.

Widow and the Judge

A widow needed some help but the judge refused to grant her justice. She kept asking until the judge finally helped her. Sometimes we have to pray over and over again, Jesus said.

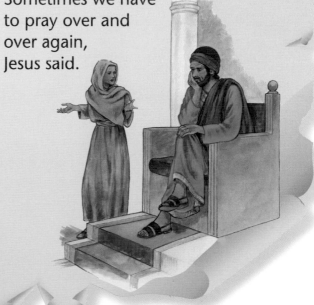

A B C D E F G H I J K L M N O P Q R S T U V W X Y Z

patience
If you wait, even if it is hard, you show that you have **patience.**

Patriarch
The one who starts and rules a tribe or family. Abraham, Isaac, and Jacob were **patriarchs.**

Paul
Paul was an apostle. He was an important teacher who wrote many letters to churches to explain how to be a Christian. Some of these letters are in the New Testament.

peace
Peace is when there is no fighting or bad feelings. The word was also used to greet others and wish them well.

peace offering
A gift to show thanks or love. In the Old Testament, people gave a **peace offering** to God by sacrificing an animal.

peacock
A large, colorful bird.

pearl
A white, shiny stone that is created by an oyster. **Pearls** are used to make jewelry.

Pentateuch
The first five books of the Old Testament, also called the Torah or the Books of the Law.

Pentecost
A feast celebrating the harvest, held 50 days after Passover begins. On the first **Pentecost** after Jesus went back to heaven, the Holy Spirit came to live in believers.

perfume
A sweet-smelling oil or lotion used to cover up bad smells or to enjoy.

perish
To be lost or destroyed. **Perish** often means to die.

perplexed
To be confused or puzzled. When Jesus died many of his followers were **perplexed.**

Persia

A large empire from the Old Testament time in present-day Iran. Esther was queen of **Persia.**

pertain

About or belonging to. Faith **pertains** to the Kingdom of God.

perverse

Wrong or evil. People in the city of Sodom were **perverse.**

pervert

To turn away from the right thing. She **perverted** the truth.

pestilence

A sickness that spreads quickly to many people. Also called a plague.

Peter

A fisherman who became the best known of the 12 disciples and a leader in the early church.

pharaoh

The ruler in Egypt was called **pharaoh.**

Pharisee

A group of very religious Jews. Jesus often said the **Pharisees** followed the rules but did not love God.

Philemon

A wealthy Christian. Paul asked him to forgive one of his servants and treat him like a brother. **Philemon** is a book in the New Testament.

Philip

One of the 12 disciples. Another **Philip** was one of the first deacons.

Philippians

A New Testament book Paul wrote to the Christians in the city of Philippi.

A B C D E F G H I J K L M N O P Q R S T U V W X Y Z

THE TEN PLAGUES ON EGYPT

In the book of Exodus, the Hebrews were slaves in Egypt. When Moses told their ruler, pharaoh, to let them go, he refused. So God sent ten terrible **plagues** until pharaoh freed the Hebrews. Here are the ten **plagues**:

1. water to blood

All the streams, rivers, and ponds were turned to blood. Even the water in pots and pitchers turned to blood.

2. frogs

Frogs came up from the rivers into all the houses, even into the bedrooms and kitchens.

3. gnats or lice

There were so many gnats and lice they were like dust in the streets.

4. flies

Then flies swarmed around the people and in their homes.

5. sick livestock

The cows, camels, sheep, and other farm animals got sick and died.

6. boils

The people got boils all over their skin.

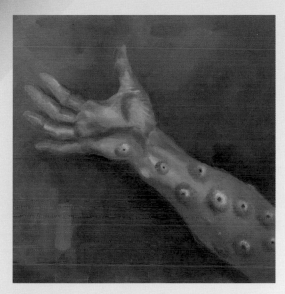

7. thunder and hail

Then there was a terrible hailstorm, which destroyed many of the crops.

8. locusts

The crops that survived were eaten by locusts, which are large grasshoppers.

9. darkness

It turned dark for three days.

10. death of firstborn

Finally, the oldest child in every house died in the night, along with the firstborn animals. Even then, when pharaoh finally let the people go, his army followed them to destroy them. But God drowned pharaoh and his whole army in the Red Sea. You can read the story of the plagues in Exodus, chapters 7 to 12.

A B C D E F G H I J K L M N O P Q R S T U V W X Y Z

Philistines

A tribe that lived in Palestine before the Hebrews. The story of them fighting the Hebrews is told in the book of Judges. Goliath was a **Philistine.**

piety

Respecting God so much you do your best to obey him.

pigs

Hebrews were not allowed to eat the meat of **pigs,** including bacon or ham. **Pigs** were also called swine.

Pilate

A Roman governor who ordered soldiers to crucify Jesus.

pillar

A post that helps hold up the roof. Can also refer to something that looks like a post, such as a pile of stones.

pine

A kind of tree. Can also mean to wish for something or someone.

pinnacle

The highest point or very top of a building.

pitch

To set up a tent. Also tar used to seal a boat.

plague

A deadly disease or event. God sent ten **plagues** on Egypt so the pharaoh would let the Hebrews go.

plaster

A covering for walls made of smooth mud. Also a mixture of medicines spread on the skin to get rid of pain or infection.

pledge

A **pledge** is an item you give someone to prove you are serious about keeping a promise or paying a debt.

plenty

More than you need. We have **plenty** of apples.

plow

A piece of wood or metal used to loosen the ground before planting seeds.

pluck

To snatch or grab. He **plucked** the fruit off the tree.

pomp

A show. The king was crowned with much **pomp.**

pool

A natural or human-made pond used to store water.

porter

One who keeps or guards a gate or door. Also called a doorkeeper.

possessed

To be owned or controlled. Masters **possessed** their slaves.

posterity

Your children and their children are your **posterity.**

potsherd

A piece of broken pottery. He used a **potsherd** to scrape the mud off his sandal.

potter

Someone who makes pots, lamps, and dishes out of clay.

potter's field

A cemetery to bury people no one knew or cared about, usually strangers.

pound

A weight, similar to a pound today. Also an amount of money, about the amount most people would make in 100 days.

praise

To show how much we appreciate someone by thanking them and saying good things about them. Christians **praise** God.

prayer

Talking to God, asking for his help or thanking him. **Prayer** is an important part of worship.

ABCDEFGHIJKLMNOPQRSTUVWXYZ

preach

To tell or announce good news to a group of people.

precept

A lesson or a rule. She followed the **precepts** of the Law.

preserve

To keep, protect, or save. The Lord **preserves** us.

press

A tool for squeezing and collecting juice or oil from fruits. Also means to push. The people **pressed** against him.

prevail

To become strong or to defeat. The Hebrews **prevailed** against their enemies.

pride

Pride is when you trust or brag about yourself too much. Satan fell because of **pride.**

priest

Someone who worked in the temple and explained what God said.

prison

A room where prisoners are kept. In Bible times, it could also be a cave or even a hole in the ground.

prize

An award. The **prize** for the man who won the race was a crown.

proclaim

To tell or announce. Angels **proclaimed** the good news.

profane

A lack of respect for holy things. People who are critical of God and have nothing to do with him are **profane.**

promise

When you assure someone you will give or do a certain thing, you make a **promise.**

Promised Land

The land God promised to Abraham. It was also known at different times as Palestine, Israel, or Canaan.

pronounce
To say or declare. God saw everything he made and **pronounced** it good.

prophecy
Words from God, often about something he is going to do.

prophet
People who carried messages from God, mostly before the Bible was written down.

proverb
A short statement of truth that is easy to remember.

Proverbs
A book in the Old Testament that is full of **proverbs.**

providence
The way God takes care of his people by providing what they need.

province
A region of a country, usually with its own governor. Similar to a state.

prudent
Wise. A good idea is a **prudent** one.

prune
To cut back part of a plant so that fresh, new leaves and branches will grow. The small knife for doing this was a **pruning** hook.

psalm
A song.

Psalms
A collection of prayers, poems, and songs in the Old Testament. Many of them were written by King David.

publican
A tax collector who worked for the Romans.

A B C D E F G H I J K L M N O P Q R S T U V W X Y Z

publish
To tell everyone. To proclaim.

puffed up
To be full of pride, showing off and not thinking you can fail.

pure
Clean. Without any marks or flaws.

purge
To take away any bad part.

purify
To make pure or clean.

purple
A color often worn by a king. It was very expensive to make clothes this color.

quail
A small bird that often traveled in large groups.

quake
To shake. The people were frightened when the earth began to **quake.**

quarter
If you divide something into four equal parts, each part is called a **quarter.** Also refers to a corner or side of a building or city.

queen
The king's wife. Kings in the Old Testament often had more than one wife, but only one was the **queen.**

quench
To put out. You can **quench** a fire or a thirst.

quiver
A case to carry arrows. Can also mean to shake slightly. She **quivered** in the cool air.

R

rabbi

A Hebrew word for teacher. Jesus was called **Rabbi.**

Rachel

Jacob's favorite wife. Her sons were Benjamin and Joseph.

rail

To yell at someone, saying things that are unkind.

raiment

Clothing. They wore fine **raiment.**

rainbow

A brightly colored arc in the sky. God said the **rainbow** showed he would never again destroy the whole world in a flood.

ram

A male goat. A **ram's** horn was used to call people together for worship or battle. This horn is also called a shofar.

rampart

A wall built up to surround and protect soldiers.

rank

A line or row of soldiers.

ransom

An amount paid to free a slave or save a life. Jesus gave his life as a **ransom** for our lives.

rash

To speak or act quickly, before thinking about what might happen.

realm

A kingdom. The good king cared for everyone in his **realm.**

reap

To pick or harvest. They went into the field to **reap** the grain.

A B C D E F G H I J K L M N O P Q R S T U V W X Y Z

rebuke

To disapprove of what someone does and tell them it is wrong. He **rebuked** his brother for lying.

reckon

To consider or count. The master **reckoned** the slave to be free.

reconcile

To restore or renew. After the argument, the friends were **reconciled.**

record

The story of what happened, often written. The Bible is a **record** of what God has done.

redeem

To buy back or pay a price for something you used to own. The man **redeemed** the field he once owned.

Red Sea

A large body of water between Africa and Asia. The Hebrews crossed the **Red Sea** when they left Egypt.

reed

A thin stalk that grows in shallow water. **Reeds** were used to make baskets or paper.

refrain

If you stop yourself from doing something, you **refrain** from it.

Rehoboam

A king of Judah, grandson of King David. He charged such high taxes that ten of the tribes rebelled, dividing the kingdom.

reign

To rule or act as a king. A king **reigns** over his people.

remnant

What remains. After the nation was destroyed, a **remnant** of people was left.

rend

To pull or tear apart. When people were sad, they would **rend** their clothes.

render

To pay or return what belongs to someone else.

repent

To turn away from. The people **repented** of their sins.

report

To tell others what happened.

reproach

To tell someone you disagree with that what he or she did or said was wrong.

reprobate

Someone who has been rejected because of their wrong actions or attitudes.

reprove

To correct. To **reprove** someone is to correct them.

resist

Oppose or fight against. God will **resist** the proud.

respect

If we show others that we like them or appreciate them, we show them **respect.**

restore

To restore something is to make it the way it was before. After the city was destroyed, Nehemiah **restored** the walls.

resurrection

When someone who was dead is made alive again. Christians celebrate the **resurrection** of Jesus at Easter.

Reuben

One of Jacob's 12 sons and the leader of one of the 12 tribes of Israel.

reveal

To uncover or show something that was hidden.

Revelation

A book in the New Testament that reveals the future.

reverence

To honor or bow down before someone to show respect.

revile

To insult someone is to **revile** them.

A B C D E F G H I J K L M N O P Q R S T U V W X Y Z

revive
Make alive. Can also mean to refresh or make new.

revolt
To rebel or reject. The people **revolted** against the king.

reward
To give something because of a good or bad action. The king **rewarded** them with gold.

riddle
Something hard to understand, like a question or proverb. Samson asked his enemies to solve a **riddle.**

righteous
To be right with God by obeying him is to be **righteous.**

rod
A long stick for walking. Could also be used to defend yourself or punish someone.

Romans
People from Rome. Paul wrote a letter to Christians in Rome, which is a book in the New Testament.

Rome
Rome was the capital city of the empire that ruled the Hebrews when Jesus was alive.

root
The part of the plant that is underground. Also used in the Bible to refer to where something comes from. Jesus was from the **root** of David.

S

Sabbath
Saturday. God commanded the Hebrews not to work on the **Sabbath** so they could worship him.

sacrifice

To offer something in worship. Hebrews would **sacrifice** animals to show they were sorry for their sins. Christians believe Jesus is the **sacrifice** who takes away their sins.

salvation

Safety. Delivered from evil or disaster. The Lord is our **salvation.**

Samaria

The northern kingdom of Israel was called **Samaria** by the time Jesus lived.

Samson

One of the judges. He was the strongest man in the Bible.

Samuel

The last judge. He anointed Saul and later David to be kings of Israel. There are two books in the Old Testament that tell his story and have his name.

sanctify

To set apart for God's use.

sapphire

A hard, clear blue stone used for jewelry and decoration.

Satan

The devil, or the evil one. He is an angel who became an enemy of God.

Saul

The first king of Israel. Also the name of the Apostle Paul before God changed it to Paul.

Savior

One who saves. In the New Testament, it refers to God and to Jesus.

scale

Scales were used to weigh something by balancing it against a set weight. A **scale** is also a thin, flaky covering on some kinds of fish.

A B C D E F G H I J K L M N O P Q R S T U V W X Y Z

scapegoat
A live goat over which the high priest listed the sins of the people. The goat was then led out into the desert to take away the sins of the people.

scorpion
A kind of spider with a poisonous stinger on a long, narrow tail.

scourge
To whip as a punishment, usually in front of others. Also a kind of whip.

scroll
A book made of paper or leather rolled up around sticks at both ends. The priest would read from a **scroll.**

Selah
A word used to mean a pause or a change in music. Often found in the psalms.

sepulcher
A cave cut out of rock to bury people in when they died.

seraphim
A kind of angel with six wings. **Seraphim** stand around the throne in heaven praising God.

sermon
A speech about what God wants. Jesus gave the **Sermon** on the Mount.

serpent
A snake.

servant
In the New Testament, a **servant** was usually a slave. He or she was owned by another person and worked for him.

sheaf
A bundle of grain, while it is still on the stalk. Farmers left a few **sheaves** in the field for poor people.

sheep
An animal used for food, clothing, and milk. Many people owned **sheep.**

shekel
A very small weight. Also a coin made of gold or silver that weighed as much as a shekel.

shepherd
One who takes care of sheep.

ship
A large boat. The Hebrews did not build large **ships,** but other countries built them for trade and war.

show bread
Twelve loaves of bread that were placed in the temple every week to remind people that God took care of them.

silver
A rare metal of great value. It was used as money or to make jewelry, candlesticks, dishes, trumpets, and other special items.

Simon
One of the 12 disciples of Jesus. His brother Andrew was also a disciple.

sin
Sin is doing something God said not to do or not doing something he did say to do. Telling a lie is a **sin.**

Sinai
A mountain in the Bible where God gave Moses the Ten Commandments. Also the name of the desert where the mountain is.

snare
A trap made with rope to catch birds and animals.

sop
A small piece of bread.

sovereign
One with complete power and control. God is our **sovereign.**

sow
To plant a crop. The farmer **sows** the seed.

span
The distance between the tips of your thumb and little finger when they are stretched out is a **span.**

spirit
The part of someone you can't touch but that makes him or her alive. God's **spirit** is called the Holy Spirit.

A B C D E F G H I J K L M N O P Q R S T U V W X Y Z

staff

A long, straight stick used to lean on when walking. Also used to clear a path or hit an attacking animal.

Stephen

One of the first deacons. **Stephen** was the first person to be killed because he followed Jesus.

steward

Someone who takes care of another person's money or things.

subject

To be obedient to or under the control of someone. People are **subject** to the king.

suffer

To be in pain or trouble. Sometimes means to allow or permit.

supplication

To ask or pray.

swaddling clothes

When babies are born, they are often wrapped tightly in a blanket. In Bible times, the blanket was called **swaddling clothes.**

swine

Pigs. Hebrews were not allowed to eat **swine.**

sycamore

A kind of tree with branches that spread out wide. It is easy to climb. Zacchaeus climbed a **sycamore** so he could see Jesus.

synagogue

After the destruction of the original temple, the places where Hebrews gathered to worship and study the Law.

T

tabernacle

A special tent. Before Solomon built the temple, Hebrews worshipped in a **tabernacle** that could be moved from place to place.

tablet
A flat surface for writing, usually made of clay.

talent
A weight, equal to about 75 pounds today. Also an amount of money, based on that weight in gold or silver. It would take years for a worker to earn a **talent.**

tanner
Someone who makes leather from animal skins.

tares
Weeds. A farmer had to separate the wheat from the **tares.**

tarry
To wait or stay behind. We will **tarry** at home.

tassel
A twisted cord fastened to the bottom of clothing or other articles as a decoration.

tax
An amount of money collected by the government or the temple.

teach
To help someone understand. Jesus was a great **teacher.**

tempest
A large storm.

temple
A place to worship God. King Solomon built the **temple** in Jerusalem.

temptation
A desire to do something bad.

Ten Commandments
Ten rules for living that were given to Moses by God. They were carved in stone by God's own finger.

tent
A home made of poles, ropes, and animal skins that could be moved from place to place. Abraham lived in a **tent.**

terrible
Something so bad we are afraid of it or feel awful about it.

testify
To tell about something you saw.

thanksgiving
Thanking God for what he does for us.

Thessalonians
Two books in the New Testament. They are letters the Apostle Paul wrote to the Christians in a Greek city called Thessalonica.

thicket
A thick section of trees or bushes that may have thorns.

thief
Someone who steals things is a **thief.**

thistle
A plant with many small thorns.

Thomas
One of the 12 disciples of Jesus. He was a twin. He had trouble believing that Jesus was alive after he had been dead.

thorn
A sharp point on a plant that can stick in your clothes or skin.

throng
A crowd. The **throng** gathered around Jesus.

tidings
News. What **tidings** do you bring?

Tigris
A large river near where Abraham was born. It is in the country we now call Iraq.

till
To loosen the dirt around a plant.

Timothy
A friend and helper of the Apostle Paul who was like a son to him. Paul wrote two letters to **Timothy** that are books in the New Testament.

tithe
To give one of every ten things you have to God. If you have ten dollars and give one dollar to the church, that is a **tithe.**

TOOLS

Tools make tasks easier. Many early tools from Bible times have been discovered by archaeologists.

awl

Holes were made with a sharp pointed piece of stone, bone, or metal called an **awl.**

ax

A tool used to chop down trees or even cut stone. Smaller versions, called chisels, were used to trim wood and stone.

bellows

Animals skins were used to make bags with small clay openings. Air could be forced through these **bellows** to make fire so hot it could melt or soften metal. Then the metal could be made into tools or weapons.

hammer

At first these were just stones used for pounding, but handles were added and eventually the head was made of iron.

hoe

Hard ground was sometimes loosened with a piece of stone or metal on the end of a stick called a **hoe.** Also called a mattock, it was used to dig, too.

knife

Short **knives** were made of hard stone, called flint, early in Bible times. Later they were made of iron or bronze.

loom

Cloth was made from wool or flax woven on a **loom.** Picks or combs made of bone or wood were used to create patterns in the cloth.

plow

A piece of wood or metal pulled behind an ox or donkey was called a **plow.** It was used to loosen the ground before planting seeds.

sickle

A curved blade with a short handle. Sometimes the blade was made of bone. It was used to cut grain in the field.

winnowing fork

This was a rake made of sticks fastened to a handle. It was used to separate the grain from the rest of the plant, called chaff.

Titus

A pastor who helped the Apostle Paul. Paul wrote him a letter that is a book in the New Testament.

token

Something given as a promise, usually a gift. He gave her a ring as a **token** of his love.

tomb

A place to bury someone when they die. In the New Testament, this was usually a small cave that was covered with a large stone.

Torah

Torah means direction from God. Also the first five books of the Bible.

tortoise

A kind of turtle.

tower

A tall building in a palace, fort, or field that was used to watch for enemies or thieves.

tradition

Something we do because we did it before and have been doing it that way for a long time.

train

The lowest part of the back of a robe. To have a long **train** meant you were wealthy.

transgression

Crossing a line. This usually means disobeying a law or rule.

travail

Hard and painful work.

travel

To go from one place to another. **Travel** was often difficult because of thieves and wild animals.

tread

To walk over something.

treasure

Something so important you guard or hide it. This does not always mean something you can touch. You can also **treasure** something in your heart or mind.

Tree of Knowledge

A special tree in the Garden of Eden. God told Adam and Eve not to eat the fruit of this tree, but they did anyway.

Tree of Life

A special tree in the Garden of Eden. The fruit made you live forever. Now the tree is in heaven.

trial

A test. Also when a judge decides if you did wrong and should be punished.

tribes of Israel

The families of Jacob's sons became the 12 **tribes of Israel.** God changed Jacob's name to Israel.

tribulation

Great trouble caused by other people or events.

tribute

A tax paid to the rulers of another country that defeated your own.

triumph

A victory. Also to shout or sing when you defeat an enemy.

trough

A long narrow box or ditch to hold food for animals.

trust

Depend on or believe in. We **trust** God.

twilight

The time after the sun goes down but before it is completely dark.

unclean

That which is dirty and unusable. In the Old Testament, certain foods, actions, or diseases made someone **unclean.** They had to leave the camp or wait a certain amount of time before they could go back into the tabernacle or temple.

unity

When everyone agrees.

A B C D E F G H I J K L M N O P Q R S T U V W X Y Z

unleavened
Bread made without yeast is **unleavened.** This makes it flat and hard.

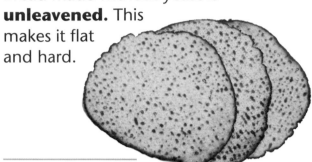

unsearchable
Something you are not able to understand because it is so big and wonderful is **unsearchable.**

uphold
To support or lift up. God **upholds** his people.

Upper Room
A room where Jesus had his last meal with his disciples.

upright
Standing straight. Also doing the right thing. He was an **upright** man.

uproar
A loud noise, usually caused by a large group of people.

Ur
The city where Abraham lived before God told him to go to Canaan.

usury
Loaning someone money but expecting them to pay back a lot more than they borrowed. This was forbidden in the Bible.

utter
Speak. Do not **utter** a word. Can also mean complete. That is **utter** foolishness.

vain
Empty or useless. That was a **vain** effort.

valiant
Brave. King David's army had many **valiant** men.

vanity
Something without value or purpose.

vessel
A pot or jar, usually made of clay.

vile
Filthy. Very dirty.

vinegar
Sour grape juice.

vineyard
A field for growing grapes. It often had a wall around it to keep out animals and thieves.

viper
A kind of snake. Its bite is filled with poison.

visage
Face or appearance. Her **visage** was very sad.

vision
A special message from God. It sometimes came in a dream.

void
Empty, with no shape.

vow
A promise, usually to God.

W

wages
Pay. Something earned by working.

wagon
A cart for carrying things. **Wagons** in the Bible usually had two wheels.

wail
A long, sad cry, usually made when someone dies.

walk
In the New Testament, this sometimes means the way you live, not just taking steps. We **walk** in love.

wall
A thick, high **wall** of stone or brick was built around a city to keep out enemies.

A B C D E F G H I J K L M N O P Q R S T U V W X Y Z

WEAPONS

Weapons made of metal appeared during the time of the Judges in the Old Testament. The **weapons** soldiers used to fight or protect themselves with changed over time, but the basic ones still worked the same way.

battle-axe

Like a sword, a **battle-axe** was used when soldiers were fighting very closely. This weapon started as a club, but later a blade was added. It was also called a mace.

bow and arrow

A **bow** was made from layers of wood or animal horns. An **arrow** was made from a thin wood pole with a metal tip. Soldiers carried **arrows** in a case called a quiver.

breastplate

A shield warriors wore on their chest that was made of heavy leather or metal.

chariot

A horse-drawn cart with two wheels. **Chariots** often held two warriors, one to hold a shield and one to shoot arrows or throw javelins.

helmet

A covering to protect the head in battle. The soldier wore a **helmet.**

shield

A handheld cover made of leather or metal. Soldiers used **shields** to protect themselves in battle. Also called a buckler.

sling

A short cord with a pouch used to throw a stone a great distance. Both shepherds and soldiers used **slings** as weapons. David used a **sling** to kill Goliath.

spear

A sharp pole used in battle. A short **spear** was called a javelin. It could be thrown a longer distance.

sword

Swords were either sharp on one side, for cutting, or both sides, for stabbing. A short **sword** was called a dagger.

ware
Something for sale. The shopkeeper laid out his **wares.**

watch
A group of soldiers guarding something. Also the amount of time they spent on guard.

wax
Bees make and use **wax** to build their nest, or honeycomb. Also means to grow or become.

wean
When a child no longer gets milk from his or her mother, he or she is **weaned.**

weave
To make cloth from many threads.

wedding
A party that is held when a man and woman get married. In Bible times, this party might last for several days.

welfare
The feeling of being completely cared for and happy. God seeks our **welfare.**

well
A hole, usually dug by hand, to find or store water.

wheat
A grain used to make bread.

wheel
Wheels in the Bible were similar to wagon **wheels** today, made from wood with spokes.

whelp
A young animal, usually a dog. Could also be a young lion.

whirlwind
Any strong or destructive wind.

whole
Complete and well. Healthy.

wicked
Evil or wrong. The king was a very **wicked** man.

widow
The wife of a man who died. In Bible times, life was very difficult for a **widow** if she had no family to take care of her.

A B C D E F G H I J K L M N O P Q R S T U V W X Y Z

WOMEN IN THE BIBLE

The Bible describes many important women. Here are just a few:

Deborah

A prophetess and judge in Israel who helped an army commander named Barak. She also wrote a famous song.

Delilah

Samson's girlfriend. Samson was one of the judges. She had his hair cut and turned him over to the Philistines, enemies of Israel.

Esther

A young Jewish woman who became queen of Persia and risked her life to save her people.

Hannah

The mother of the prophet Samuel. She prayed for him to be born and then dedicated him to serve God when he was very young.

Mary

The mother of Jesus. An angel told her she would have a baby who would save the world. Her cousin Elizabeth was the mother of John the Baptist.

Miriam

The sister of Moses. She hid him from pharaoh when he was a baby and later helped him lead the Hebrews to freedom from Egypt.

Rahab

A woman from Jericho who helped the Hebrews by hiding two of their spies. When the Hebrews destroyed her city, she was saved.

Rebekah

The wife of Isaac and the mother of Jacob and Esau. She "inquired of the Lord" about God's place for her son Jacob.

Ruth

A woman from Moab. She moved to Israel with her mother-in-law, Naomi, and became the great-grandmother of King David. The book of **Ruth** is in the Old Testament.

Sarah

The wife of Abraham and the mother of Isaac. She gave birth to Isaac when she was very old.

A B C D E F G H I J K L M N O P Q R S T U V W X Y Z

wilderness
Land that is too dry or rough to farm.

wind
The movement of air. Winds had different effects: The north wind brought rain and the east wind brought storms. Also means spirit.

winepress

A hole cut in a rock, used for pressing juice from grapes. Wine was often pressed by people stomping on the grapes with their feet.

winnow

To separate the grain from the chaff. The chaff was the stems and other parts that were not used for making flour.

wisdom
Knowing what to do. In the Bible, **wisdom** begins with worshipping and obeying God. Someone who does this is **wise.**

wither
To dry up or make unusable. Jesus healed a man with a **withered** hand.

witness
To tell what you saw or know.

woe
Deep sorrow or trouble.

womb
The place in a woman's body where a baby grows.

wonder
Something great or amazing. A miracle.

worm
A crawling creature with no bones. It sometimes means someone who is weak.

worship
To praise, obey, and enjoy God, often by praying and singing.

wrath
Anger, especially God's anger toward sin.

A B C D E F G H I J K L M N O P Q R S T U V W X Y Z

X

Xerxes
A king of Persia. He married a young Hebrew woman named Esther.

Y

yoke
A wooden frame that joins two animals so they can pull a wagon or plow together.

Z

Zacchaeus
A tax collector who climbed a tree to see Jesus, who was in a crowd of people. **Zacchaeus** was a short man.

zeal
Eagerness and excitment.

Zechariah
One of the kings of Israel. Also a prophet who encouraged the Hebrews to rebuild the temple in the Old Testament book of **Zechariah.**

Zephaniah
The Old Testament book of **Zephaniah** warns the Hebrews not to worship other gods. It was written by the prophet **Zephaniah.**

Zion
The name of a fort in Jerusalem. The name came to mean both the city of Jerusalem and heaven.

A B C D E F G H I J K L M N O P Q R S T U V W X Y Z